The Tortoise and the Hare

Read each sentence. Write the word from the box that means the same as the word or words in **pink** print.

animals	plods	story	message
reached	start	noisy	sleep

1. "The Tortoise and the Hare" is an old **tale**.
2. In it, the two very different **creatures** race each other.
3. The hare quickly hops off at the **beginning** of the race.
4. The tortoise **slowly moves** along.
5. Since he is so far ahead, the hare decides to eat and **nap**.
6. After awhile, the hare wakes up to **loud** cheers.
7. The tortoise has **arrived at** the Finish Line.
8. The **moral** of the story is *Slow and steady wins the race.*

Twins

Read each sentence. Fill in the blank with the word from the box that means the opposite of the word in **orange** print.

summer	tiny	slow	father	different	left	late	sister

1. Ari and Livia are twin **brother** and ______________.

2. They look **alike** but they are ______________.

3. Ari writes with his **right** hand. Livia is __________-handed.

4. Livia likes **huge** animals. Ari likes __________ ones.

5. Ari's favorite season is **winter**.

   Livia likes ______________ best.

6. Livia likes to go down the water slide really **fast**.

   Ari likes to go down __________.

7. Ari likes to wake up **early**. Livia likes to sleep in__________.

8. Both kids love their **mother** and ______________.

ari xox
oxo Livia

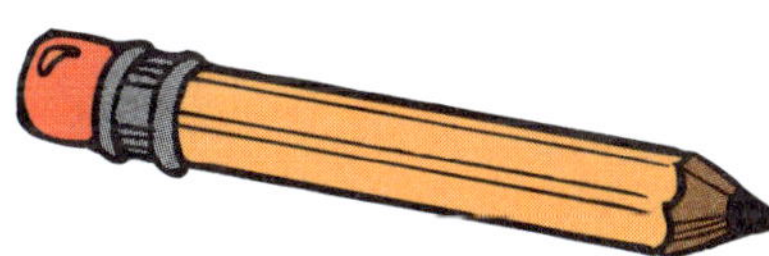

Write It Right

Write the right word to finish each sentence.

1. Serena ____________ her book.
2. It was a story about a big ____________ dog named Clifford.

for / four

3. Timmy has ____________ brothers.
4. He drew a picture ____________ one of them.

new / knew

5. Lisa got a ____________ bike for her birthday.
6. She ____________ her grandma was buying it.

won / one

7. Raul ____________ the spelling contest.
8. He was the only ____________ who could spell *Wednesday*.

pair / pear

9. Molly ate a ____________ for lunch.
10. She also had a ____________ of cherries.

their / there

11. Chris and Sean are standing over ____________ .
12. They are waiting for ____________ dad.

We All Fall Down

Some words, like *fall*, have more than one meaning.

fall 1. to come down from a higher place; drop
2. season of the year; autumn
3. waterfall (usually written as a plural—*falls*)

Read each sentence. Decide if the word *fall* or *falls* matches the first, second, or third meaning. Write **1**, **2**, or **3** in the circle.

○ "Ashes, ashes, we all **fall** down."

○ Leaves change color in the **fall**.

○ If you **fall** on the mat, you won't get hurt.

○ They went over the **falls** in their raft.

○ Whenever the baby **falls**, she laughs and says "Boom!"

○ My favorite time of the year is **fall**.

○ If you stand close to the **falls**, the water will spray you.

○ If enough snow **falls**, we can go sledding tomorrow.

○ You need to wear a sweatshirt on cool **fall** days.

○ If you **fall** out of that tree, you'll break a leg.

"Not" Words

The prefixes *un-*, *im-*, and *in-* mean "not."
Draw a line to match each word to its picture.

happy

unhappy

polite

impolite

correct

incorrect

possible

impossible

kind

unkind

visible

invisible

Dancer—One Who Dances

The suffixes *-er* and *-or* mean "one who." Write each word from the box under the matching picture. Circle the suffix.

painter	actor	farmer	sculptor	dancer
doctor	teacher	author	plumber	

Caribou

Read the paragraph. Answer the questions.

Caribou (CARE uh boo) are a kind of deer. They live in the cold northern areas of North America. Caribou and reindeer are the only kinds of deer whose males and females both have antlers. Caribou travel in large groups called herds. There are sometimes 10,000 caribou in the herd.

1. What is a caribou?

____

2. Where do caribou live?

____

3. How are caribou like reindeer?

____

____

4. What is the most interesting thing you learned about caribou? Explain why.

____

____

____

Headlines

A headline tells the main idea of a news story.

Read these stories. Choose the best headline from the box for each story. Write it above the story.

Headlines

Good Fairy to Visit Town
Woman Dies From Eating Many Animals
Pesky Fly Is Missing
Mice Are Having a Bad Day
Naughty Rabbit Turned Into Goon

An old woman who accidentally swallowed a fly, died from eating several other animals. Her family said she ate a spider, bird, cat, dog, goat, cow, and horse in that order to catch the fly. The horse, of course, was too much.

A naughty rabbit named Little Bunny Foo Foo was turned into a goon yesterday. He was bothering field mice all day long. The Good Fairy gave Foo three chances, but he wouldn't stop. So she changed him from a rabbit to a goon.

Animals in the News

A headline tells the main idea of a news story.

Read these stories. Choose the best headline from the box for each story. Write it above the story.

Headlines

Icebergs Are Dangerous
Humpback Whale Safely Back at Sea
Whale to Star in Show
People Rescue Oil Spill Animals
Oil Spill Kills Plants and Animals

Children and adults are helping rescue animals hurt in an oil spill. They are bathing birds, otters, seals, and other animals to clean off the oil on their feathers and fur. It is hard for the animals to swim or fly when coated with the sticky oil.

A lost humpback whale has been guided back to sea. It traveled several miles up a river away from its family. Scientists and volunteers used loud noises to help turn it around. People lined the shore to watch the whale and cheer it on as it went back to sea.

All About Flying

Read this table of contents. Then answer the questions.

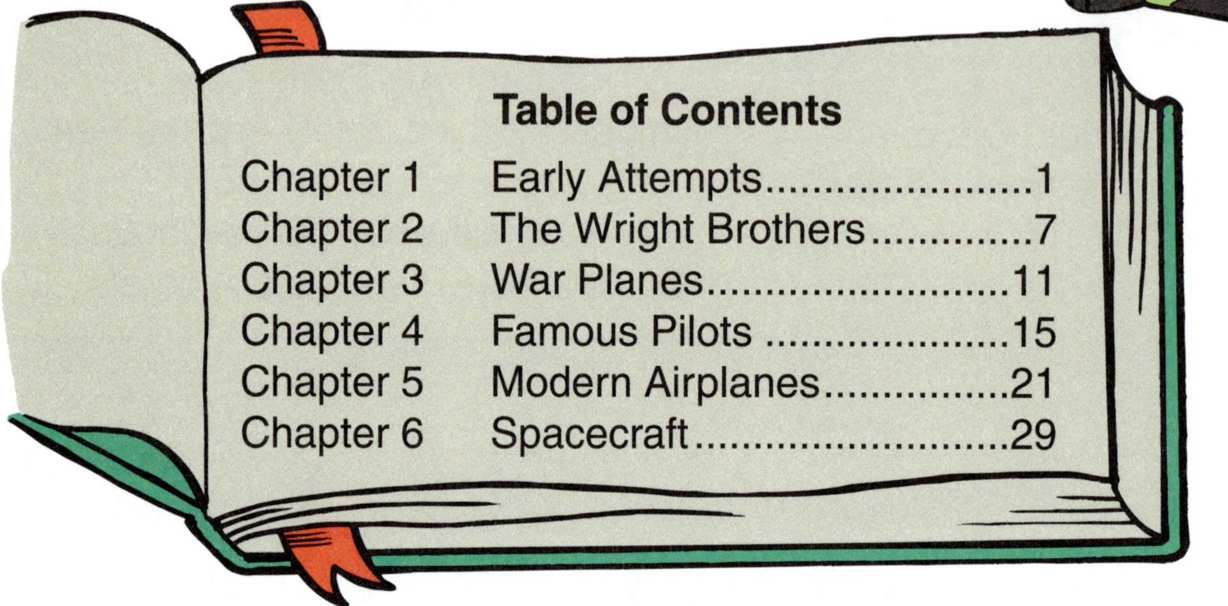

Table of Contents

A. Which chapter tells about the Wright Brothers? ________

B. On what page does the Famous Pilots chapter begin? ________

C. If you are on page 11, what are you reading about? ____________________

____

D. If you want to find out about planes you might fly in today, what is the name of the chapter you should read? ____________________

____

E. If you want to find out about the space shuttle or rockets, which chapter should you read? ____________________

F. If you are on page 4, what are you reading about? ____________________

____

Long or Short?

Read the words in each box. Decide if the word has a short or long vowel. Write the word on the correct pencil.

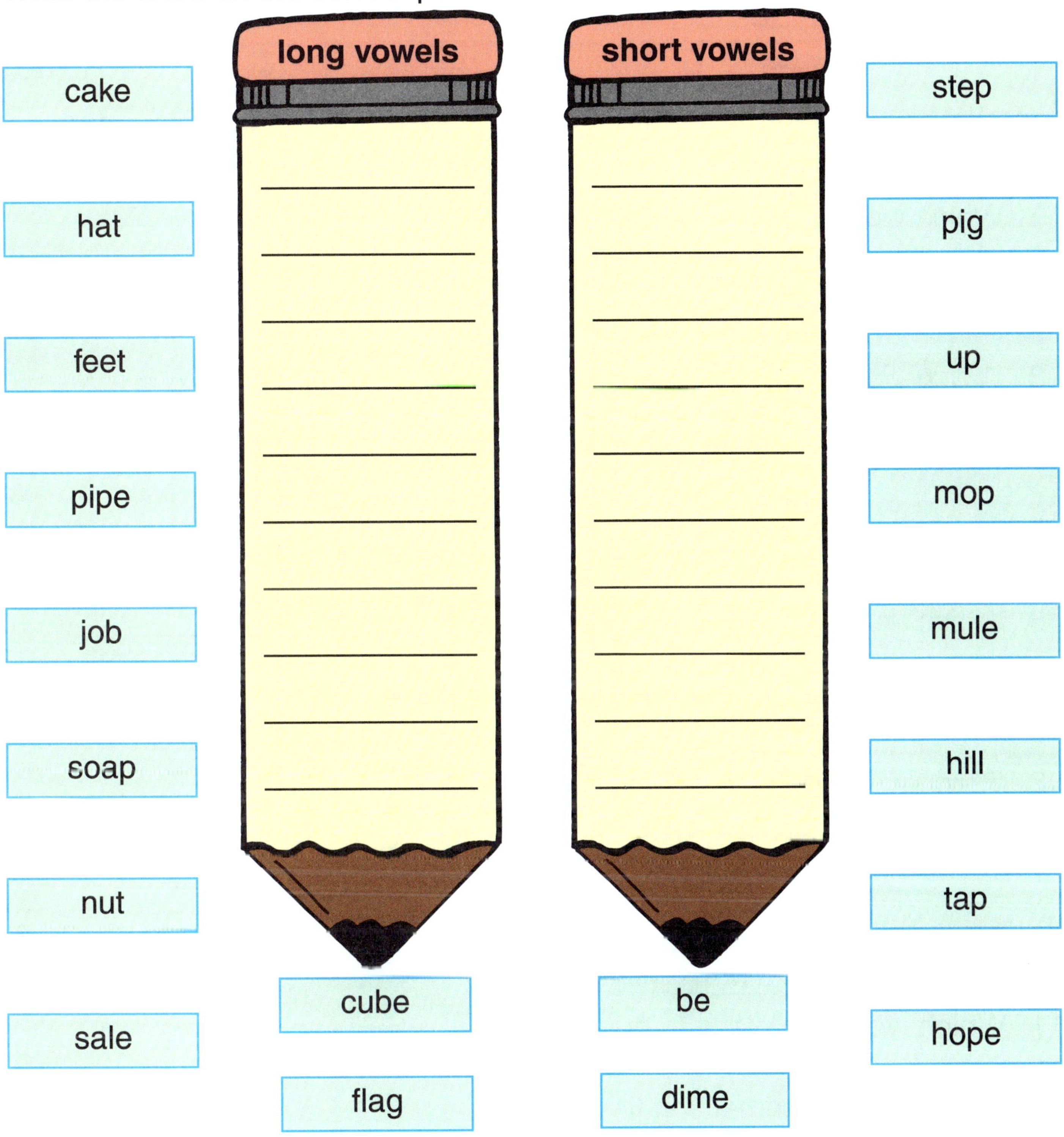

Which Word?

Write the answers on the lines. Use the words in the box.

forty	March	purple	girl	skirt	circus
market	perfume	fern	nurse	birthday	farm

1. Which word is the name of a month? ____________
2. Which word is a number? ____________
3. Which word names a color? ____________
4. Which word is something that smells good? ____________
5. Which word is a green plant? ____________
6. Which word is someone who works in a hospital? ____________
7. Which word is the opposite of *boy*? ____________
8. Which word is a place where corn grows? ____________
9. Which word is a place with clowns? ____________
10. Which word is a day to celebrate? ____________
11. Which word is a place to buy things? ____________
12. Which word is something to wear? ____________

What's Missing?

Write **ar, er, ir, or,** or **ur** to complete each word.

fork	c n	zipp
30 th ty	st	p se
t key	t tle	m
y n	ange	h se

Book or Boot?

Read each word below. Decide if the word has the **oo** sound as in **book** or the **oo** sound as in **boot**. Write the words in the correct box.

tool
took
moon
school
hook
room
good
foot
tooth
hood
roof
cook
soon
wood
pool
stood
shook
look
mood
zoo

book

____________ ____________

____________ ____________

____________ ____________

____________ ____________

____________ ____________

boot

____________ ____________

____________ ____________

____________ ____________

____________ ____________

____________ ____________

Sentence Fun

Write a sentence with each of the words below.

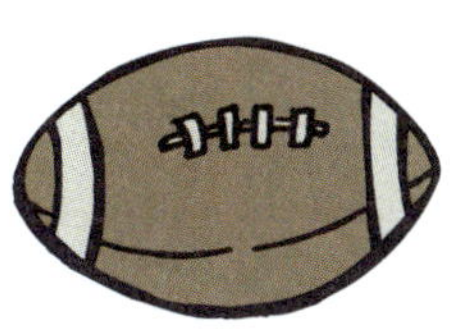

1. football ______________________________

2. bloom ______________________________

3. shook ______________________________

4. stood ______________________________

5. book ______________________________

6. hook ______________________________

7. moon ______________________________

8. cookie ______________________________

9. brook ______________________________

10. good ______________________________

Cow or Crow?

Read each word below. Decide if the word has the **ow** sound as in **crow** or the **ow** sound as in **cow**. Write the word on the correct list.

town	grow
clown	know
owl	blow
slow	flower
window	brown
snow	now
show	how
bowl	down
tow	shower
towel	below
throw	crown

cow	crow
______	______
______	______
______	______
______	______
______	______
______	______
______	______
______	______
______	______
______	______
______	______
______	______

Fun With Riddles

Read each riddle. Find the answer in the word box and write it on the line.

1. You can plant a seed in me. I will help it grow.

   What am I?

   ____

2. I am the sound that comes out of your mouth when you speak.

   What am I?

   ____

3. I am the opposite of a girl.

   What am I?

   ____

4. You can play with me. I can be a ball, a kite, or a doll.

   What am I?

   ____

5. You can buy things with me. I am made of metal.

   What am I?

   ____

6. I am the sharp end on a pencil.

   What am I?

   ____

Write your own riddles for these words.

7. noise ____

   ____

8. boil ____

   ____

Space Is the Place

Number each group of words in alphabetical order.

A.	B.	C.	
___ Jupiter	___ Uranus	___ Mercury	
___ gravity	___ Neptune	___ moon	
___ galaxy	___ universe	___ meteor	

D.		E.	F.
___ Saturn		___ rings	___ crater
___ satellite		___ rocket	___ comet
___ Sun		___ rotate	___ spins

G.	H.		I.
___ Earth	___ star		___ ocean
___ eclipse	___ system		___ Orion
___ energy	___ solar		___ orbit

	J.	K.	L.
	___ planet	___ astronaut	___ space
	___ phase	___ air	___ Sputnik
	___ Pluto	___ Apollo	___ shuttle

Book Bright

Number each group of words in alphabetical order.

A.

____ Annie
____ grandmother
____ weave

B.

____ hippos
____ George
____ Martha

C.

____ Frizzle
____ bus
____ body

D.

____ Ferdinand
____ flowers
____ fight

E.

____ Frog
____ Toad
____ friends

F.

____ Kapiti
____ Ki-pat
____ rain

G.

____ mitten
____ mouse
____ mole

H.

____ crow
____ Chibi
____ school

I.

____ Charlotte
____ Wilbur
____ web

J.

____ Patrick
____ dinosaur
____ diplodocus

K.

____ Nelson
____ Swamp
____ school

L.

____ slipper
____ stepsisters
____ Cinderella

Let's Ride!

Write the contraction for each pair of words. Take out the boldfaced letters. Put in an apostrophe. Example: should + n**o**t = shouldn't

1. 

2. 

3. 

4. 

5. 

6. 

7. 

8. 

9. 

More Than One

Add **s** to most words to make plurals.

Add **es** to words that end in **sh, ch, s,** or **x** to make them plural.

Add **s** or **es** to make plurals. Write the plural form of each word.

A. 1 house 2 _ _ _ _ _ _	**B.** 1 inch 2 _ _ _ _ _ _	**C.** 1 shell 2 _ _ _ _ _ _
D. 1 box 2 _ _ _ _ _	**E.** 1 bus 2 _ _ _ _ _	**F.** 1 line 2 _ _ _ _ _
G. 1 pen 2 _ _ _ _	**H.** 1 chair 2 _ _ _ _ _ _	**I.** 1 bush 2 _ _ _ _ _ _
J. 1 key 2 _ _ _ _	**K.** 1 fox 2 _ _ _ _ _	**L.** 1 dish 2 _ _ _ _ _ _

Late Last Night

Choose the correct word from each box. Write it on the line.

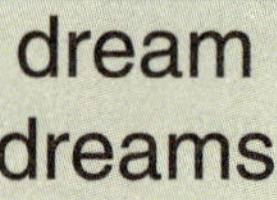

dream dreams	1. Last night I had a strange ______________.
alien aliens	2. Two ______________ knocked on my window.
bed beds	3. I sat up in my ______________ and looked.
eye eyes	4. One alien had three ______________ and four ears.
ear ears	5. The other had six eyes and one ______________.
noise noises	6. They made a strange ______________, then left.
stair stairs	7. I raced down the ______________ and ran outside.
answer answers	8. I called "Hello!" but there was no ______________.
light lights	9. Then I saw a bunch of flashing ______________ in the sky. Their spaceship flew away.

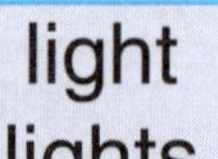

Present and Past

Draw lines to match up the present tense and past tense verbs.

Today you . . .	Yesterday you . . .	Today you . . .	Yesterday you . . .
play	went	see	lived
work	liked	get	saw
go	swam	take	knew
like	played	live	got
swim	worked	know	took
fly	called	give	thought
talk	sang	think	gave
sing	flew	tell	wanted
call	talked	come	put
are	wrote	want	told
write	were	show	came
have	made	put	asked
make	did	read	showed
say	said	ask	tried
do	had	try	read

Past or Present?

Write the correct verb from the box to finish this poem.

clopped
clops

Yesterday the horse clip-__________________,
Now it __________________ some more.

hops
hopped

Yesterday the rabbit __________________,
Now it __________________ some more.

creeps
crept

Yesterday the turtle __________________,
Now it __________________ some more.

leapt
leaps

Yesterday the bullfrog __________________,
Now it __________________ some more.

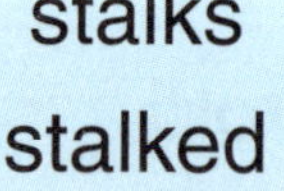

stalks
stalked

Yesterday the sly cat __________________,
Now it __________________ some more.

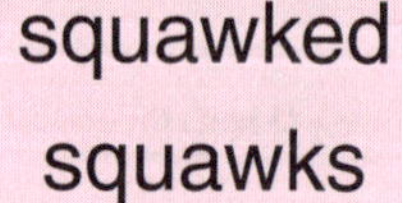

squawked
squawks

Yesterday the blackbird __________________,
Now it __________________ no more!

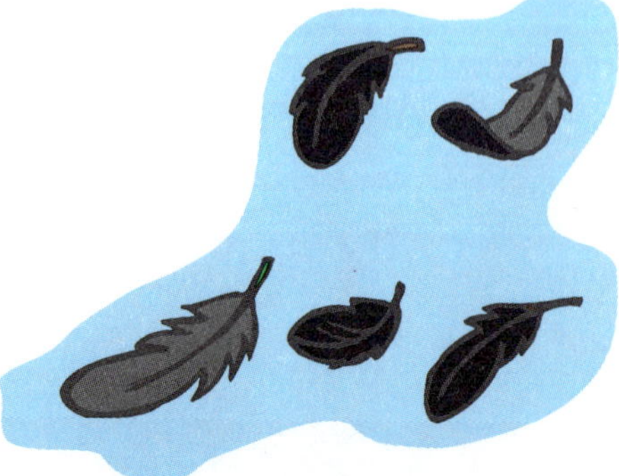

You Name It

Fill in the blanks with names of people, places, or dates. Remember to begin each with a capital letter.

1. My full name is ______________________________

____

2. I was born in the month of ______________________________
3. A good friend of mine is ______________________________
4. The name of my town or city is ______________________________

____

5. The name of my country is ______________________________

____

6. A place I would like to visit is ______________________________

____

7. The leader of my country is ______________________________

____

8. A person I admire is ______________________________

____

Totem Pole

Read each sentence.
Write a . at the end if it is a telling sentence.
Write a ? at the end if it is a question.
Write a ! at the end if it shows strong feelings.

1. Wow, that's a beautiful totem pole
2. Have you ever seen a totem pole
3. It is a tall pole carved from a log
4. Do you know what totem poles are for
5. Some totem poles tell a story or legend
6. Others are carved to honor someone
7. Who makes totem poles
8. They are carved by Native Americans of the Northwest Coast
9. The Tsimshian tribe carve totem poles
10. Where do the Tsimshian people live
11. They live in British Columbia, Canada
12. I wish I could carve a totem pole

Goodbye, Cassie!

Read each sentence.
Write a . at the end if it is a telling sentence.
Write a ? at the end if it is a question.
Write a ! at the end if it shows strong feelings.

1. Oh, no
2. My best friend, Cassie, is moving away
3. She and I have been friends since we were babies
4. Have you ever had a friend move away
5. What am I going to do
6. My parents are having a party tonight for Cassie's family

7. We may get to stay up until midnight
8. Tomorrow the moving van comes
9. How long will it take to load up their things
10. Cassie said she will write me letters
11. I can visit her next summer
12. I'll miss you, Cassie

Finally!

Circle the 10 words that are spelled wrong. Write each correctly on the line. Check your spellings with the words in the box.

1. ____________ I just lost mi first baby tooth! It
2. ____________ took a long time. Everybody I kno
3. ____________ lost a tooth in kindergarten or ferst
4. ____________ grad. But it took me until second

grade.

My parents took me to the

5. ____________ dentist last yeer. The dentist told
6. ____________ me not to woory. She said my baby
7. ____________ teeth would fall out when my uther
8. ____________ teeth were reddy to come in.

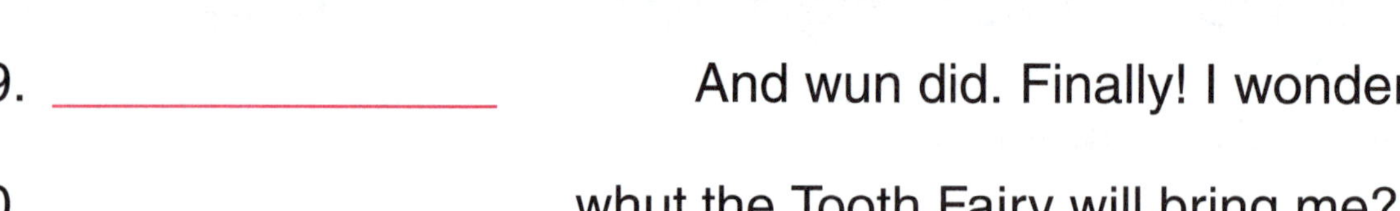

9. ____________ And wun did. Finally! I wonder
10. ____________ whut the Tooth Fairy will bring me?

first	grade	know	my	one	other	ready	what	worry	year

The First Phone

Circle the 10 words that are spelled wrong. Write each correctly on the line. Check your spellings with the words in the box.

1. ________________ Do yoo know who invented
2. ________________ the telephone? It wuz Alexander

Graham Bell. He did it over a

3. ________________ hundred yeers ago.
4. ________________ Thomas Watson helpt him.
5. ________________ He was wating in another room to
6. ________________ heer Bell's message. The first
7. ________________ words Bell spoke on the fone

were: "Mr. Watson, come here. I

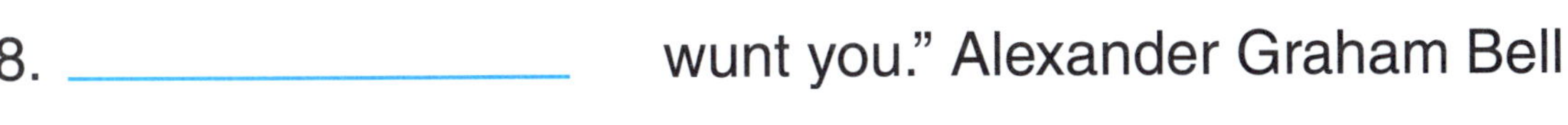

8. ________________ wunt you." Alexander Graham Bell
9. ________________ sed those words because he had
10. ________________ just spilld something on himself!

hear	helped	phone	said	spilled	waiting	want	was	years	you

Dear Eagle

If you could be any animal, which would you be? Write a friendly letter to that animal. Choose one of these topics to write about:

- [ ] why you like that animal
- [ ] what you want to learn about that animal
- [ ] how you are different from that animal

Turtles

Read these notes about turtles.
Write complete sentences using the ideas from the notes.

Turtle Notes

General
- reptiles
- cold-blooded
- hatch from eggs
- most eat both plants and animals

Body
- hard shell
- four legs
- tail
- hard beak

Some kinds
- pond turtles
- snapping turtles
- mud turtles
- sea turtles
- tortoises

Sample: Turtles are cold-blooded animals.

1. ______________________________

2. ______________________________

3. ______________________________

4. ______________________________

Answers

Page One

1. story	5. sleep
2. animals	6. noisy
3. start	7. reached
4. plods	8. message

Page Two

1. sister	5. summer
2. different	6. slow
3. left	7. late
4. tiny	8. father

Page Three

1. read	7. won
2. red	8. one
3. four	9. pear
4. for	10. pair
5. new	11. there
6. knew	12. their

Page Four

1, 2, 1, 3, 1, 2, 3, 1, 2, 1

Page Five

(boy crying)—unhappy, (boy smiling)—happy; (girl saying "Gimme!")—impolite, (girl saying "Please")—polite; (2+2=4)—correct, (2+2=5)—incorrect; (boy lifting barbell)—possible, (baby lifting barbell)—impossible; (boys sharing a cone)—kind, (boy upsetting a cone)—unkind; (hat and tie in midair)—invisible, (boy wearing hat and tie)—visible

Page Six

dancer, farmer, author
doctor, painter, teacher
plumber, actor, sculptor
The suffixes should be circled.

Page Seven

1. a kind of deer
2. cold northern areas of North America
3. both males and females have antlers
4. Answer varies.

Page Eight

Woman Dies From Eating Many Animals
Naughty Rabbit Turned Into Goon

Page Nine

People Rescue Oil Spill Animals
Humpback Whale Safely Back at Sea

Page Ten

A. 2
B. 15
C. War Planes
D. Modern Airplanes
E. 6
F. Early attempts at flying

Page Eleven

Order of words on each pencil may vary.
Long vowels: cake, feet, pipe, mule, soap, sale, cube, be, hope, dime
Short vowels: step, hat, pig, up, mop, job, hill, nut, tap, flag

Page Twelve

1. March	7. girl
2. forty	8. farm
3. purple	9. circus
4. perfume	10. birthday
5. fern	11. market
6. nurse	12. skirt

Page Thirteen

fork, corn, zipper
thirty, star, purse
turkey, turtle, arm
yarn, orange, horse

Page Fourteen

Order of words in each box may vary.
Book: took, hook, good, foot, hood, cook, wood, stood, shook, look
Boot: tool, moon, school, room, tooth, roof, soon, pool, mood, zoo

Page Sixteen

Cow: town, clown, owl, flower, brown, now, how, down, shower, towel, crown, power
Crow: grow, know, blow, slow, window, snow, show, bowl, tow, below, throw, glow

Page Seventeen

1. soil	4. toy
2. voice	5. coin
3. boy	6. point

Riddles will vary.

Page Eighteen

A. 3, 2, 1	G. 1, 2, 3
B. 3, 1, 2	H. 2, 3, 1
C. 1, 3, 2	I. 1, 3, 2
D. 2, 1, 3	J. 2, 1, 3
E. 1, 2, 3	K. 3, 1, 2
F. 2, 1, 3	L. 2, 3, 1

Page Nineteen

A. 1, 2, 3,	G. 1, 3, 2
B. 2, 1, 3	H. 2, 1, 3
C. 3, 2, 1	I. 1, 3, 2
D. 1, 3, 2	J. 3, 1, 2
E. 2, 3, 1	K. 1, 3, 2
F. 1, 2, 3	L. 2, 3, 1

Page Twenty

1. didn't	6. he'd
2. she's	7. we'll
3. didn't	8. who's
4. they're	9. wouldn't
5. can't	

Page Twenty-one

A. houses	G. pens
B. inches	H. chairs
C. shells	I. bushes
D. boxes	J. keys
E. buses	K. foxes
F. lines	L. dishes

Page Twenty-two

1. dream	6. noise
2. aliens	7. stairs
3. bed	8. answer
4. eyes	9. lights
5. ear	

Page Twenty-three

play—played
work—worked
go—went
like—liked
swim—swam
fly—flew
talk—talked
sing—sang
call—called
are—were
write—wrote
have—had
make—made
say—said
do—did
see—saw
get—got
take—took
live—lived
know—knew
give—gave
think—thought
tell—told
come—came
want—wanted
show—showed
put—put
read—read
ask—asked
try—tried

Page Twenty-four

clopped, clops
hopped, hops
crept, creeps
leapt, leaps
stalked, stalks
squawked, squawks

Page Twenty-six

1. (!)	7. (?)
2. (?)	8. (.)
3. (.)	9. (.)
4. (?)	10. (?)
5. (.)	11. (.)
6. (.)	12. (. or !)

Page Twenty-seven

1. (!)	7. (. or !)
2. (.)	8. (.)
3. (.)	9. (?)
4. (?)	10. (.)
5. (?)	11. (.)
6. (.)	12. (. or !)

Page Twenty-eight

1. my	6. worry
2. know	7. other
3. first	8. ready
4. grade	9. one
5. year	10. what

Page Twenty-nine

1. you	6. hear
2. was	7. phone
3. years	8. want
4. helped	9. said
5. waiting	10. spilled